## About Sara Millis of Sara's Texture Crafts

What can I say; I'm a fibre addict… I am wool obsessed and can often be found in a woolly trance playing with fibre and yarn!

So where did my obsession with wool really start? Well I trained in fashion and worked as a Fashion and Textile Designer for a few British Fashion Designers and larger brands… when I visited factories I was always taken with the complexity and ingenuity behind fabric constructions and fibre choice. When I later became a freelance consultant and started Sara's Texture Crafts as a side-line I seemed drawn to wool in particular.

Since then I have taken to many wool crafts felt making, embellishing (textile surface decoration), weaving, crochet and in particular spinning and knitting. I have also had the pleasure of meeting many fellow fibre addicts who have been so free to share their craft passions and knowledge… I think that's why I love my job so much… you meet the most fabulous people!

As Sara's Texture Crafts grew I felt compelled to give back, not only in high quality product, but also in learning and so my work became as much about beautiful product as it did about sharing and inspiring customers on how to use it. I write a blog called Crafts of Texture where I share most of my inspiration, tutorials and patterns.

I always strive to source the very best of products to sell and am continuously looking for new suppliers and methods to be able to bring my ideas to you. Currently I work with a selection of UK Farmers (locally where possible), crafts people and suppliers as well as a few overseas brands for the bigger pieces of equipment, to be able to do this. I also create a proportion of the products myself, based on my experience with fibres, yarn and various wool crafts.

If you have any questions regarding my products, or services please get in touch.

Sara x

www.sarastexturecrafts.com

# Contents

## Introduction

Lots of people have asked me about gradient spinning since the release of my gradient hand dyed tops range at www.sarastexturecrafts.com, so I thought I would write up some very simple tutorials to give you an idea of how you might spin hand dyed gradients or create your own.

For the initial stages of this series I thought we should look at the very basic types of gradient spinning, then moving on to looking at what sort of projects/garments might work in gradient spun yarn and lastly designing projects and garments around gradient spun yarn.

## What is a Hand Dyed Gradient?

A gradient is a fibre which changes in colour in a measureable way from one to another.

We start looking at hand dyed gradients, either those you make yourself, or you buy from indie dyers like myself.

It's probably wise at this point to start by considering some terminology. This will not only help you understand different types of gradients available, but also how they might look both in a braid or knit up.

Many sellers, myself included tag these types of hand dyes with the loose term 'Gradient', even though there are differences in the types of gradient available... why you ask? Well, it's really about our ability to sell to a wider audience. For example we are aiming ourselves at advanced spinners as well as those who are beginner spinners, or those who are shopping on larger forums such as Etsy, where there is so much to choose from and we want our listings to be easily found. So using a generic term helps. However, we do understand as you do (or I hope you will by the end of this series) that there are nuances between colour changing techniques.

There are essentially two terms to have in mind when selecting your gradient project;

### True Gradients

A **'True Gradient'** is a dye technique that starts with one colour at one end and then slowly and subtly morphs into a secondary colour at the other end.

It can be a tonal gradient, which is a high saturate to a lower saturate of one colour, or two or more different colours in one braid.

## Progressive Gradients

A **'Progressive Gradient'** is a dye technique that starts with one colour at one end and then suddenly changes into a secondary colour at the other end.

Both types of gradient can have more than one colour, but for the purpose of our experiments I have kept it simple and used two fairly different colours.

Here they are spun up;

5

## Easy ways to spin a gradient braid

I should mention early on that I am aiming this post at the beginner spinner, those of you more advanced may wish to skip this section... although I hope you will read on just to familiarise yourself with some basics in plying.

Ok... Now there are many different ways we could choose to ply our gradient singles, if we haven't decided to keep the yarn as a single ply. Today I want to compare a basic two ply and a Navajo ply to show you how similar the results might be and to discuss why we might choose one over another.

Do you remember this true gradient I showed you earlier? Well I have spun this up for us to have a closer look at and I thought it might be an interesting experiment for you to try at home.

So I started with my braid...

I tore the gradient into thirds along the length (tearing from top to bottom), so that I could make two yarns... now of course this will not give us accuracy in our finished yarns, but for the purpose of experimentation it works fine.

Yarn 1 - The bump with the pink outer layer was spun Navajo ply (see further reading for a tutorial video recommendation).

Yarn 2 - The two remaining yellow outer layered bumps where spun into singles and then 2-plied together.

Here they are;

You can see in the skeins that there is no obvious difference... and in fact knitted up there is little difference either and this is what I would really expect. The same is true of hand dyed progressive gradients (although there may be areas of overlap if your singles aren't equal which will create some hazing. It is also true for creating your own faux gradients shown in later chapters.

So why bother experimenting? Well, in my opinion the real experiment here is about deciding on ply structure and how that creates a different handle to your knitting and therefore your choice of finished garment. So later when we start talking about designing garments you can also have in mind how plying your yarns can make a good deal of difference to the garment.

Although our experiment in terms of yardage wasn't strictly accurate (scientifically speaking), the finished swatches do show us clearly two things for our consideration in terms of finished fabric;

1. Navajo ply over 2 ply yields a shorter yardage. Therefore we would need more yarn to knit a sweater for example.

2. Navajo over two ply also creates a more 'dense' fabric. Therefore a 2 ply might be better if we want a light a floaty summer shawl for example.

Why choose Navajo ply, or a 2 ply?

Navajo ply is easier to control a gradient if you are wishing for a true gradient, or a very controlled progressive.

A two ply is an easier option if you want to merge the colours, as it's very difficult to control the way that the colours fall together during plying.

## How to make a faux gradient yarn

Creating your own gradient yarns from pre coloured fibres you already have in your stash is a great way to make your own unique look.

In this chapter we are going to look at how to make a progressive gradient and a true gradient.

Progressive Faux Gradient.

**Sara's Texture Crafts Faux Gradient Tutorial**

**Materials** from www.SarasTextureCrafts.com
3 x 25g of Merino in three different colours
spinning implement of your choosing (spindle or wheel).

**Steps -**

1.  Place your three colours in a line in an order that you find pleasing. I'm using colours **Turquoise, Purple and Fuchsia**.

2.  Pick up your first colour and start spinning... now because we are creating a swatch, I am not worried about truly consistent yarn, or aiming for a particular weight of yarn (4ply, dk, aran, etc.)

3.  When this colour is finished, join your second colour and then the third afterwards.

4. You now have a bobbin, or spindle cop full of yarn.

5. To ply this yarn and balance it (singles often bias when knit) I have chosen to Navajo ply.

When you have finished plying, let your yarn rest either on the spindle/bobbin or a niddy noddy for a day. This will help relax any areas of slight over spin. You are now able to set your yarn in the usual way.

Knit up a swatch and take a good look at how the swatch knits up. You will note that the swatch as seen in my picture above knits in very distinct wedges of colour and breaks to the next colour very abruptly... now while this is great for some projects, in others you may wish for something more subtle.

<u>True Faux Gradient.</u>

This is a simple way to make your 'faux' gradient spinning more subtle in colour transition.

**Materials** from www.SarasTextureCrafts.com
3 x 30g of Merino in three different colours
carding equipment of your choice (drum carder, or hand carders)
spinning implement of your choosing (spindle or wheel).

**Steps -**

- Place your three colours in a line in an order that you find pleasing. I'm using colours **Turquoise, Purple and Fuchsia.**

- We now need to divide our colours, in a way that will graduate from one colour to the next. I am using a very simple formula to do this;

  o Split your Turquoise colour into three smaller balls of 10g. Do the same for colours Purple and Fuchsia.

  o Lay out your balls into the following line;

    ▪ Ball 1 - Turquoise 10g

    ▪ Ball 2 - 10g Turquoise + 10g Purple (balled together). I made 2 balls here for ease of carding.

    ▪ Ball 3 - 10g Purple

    ▪ Ball 4 - 10g Purple + 10g Fuchsia (balled together). I made 2 balls here for ease of carding.

    ▪ Ball 5 - 10g Fuchsia.

- Now we need to start carding our balls of fibre... we are going to do this with all ball sets separately, including those that are to remain solid. We do this to help us keep a consistent spin. Balls 1, 3 and 5 will probably only need a light carding, whereas balls 2 and 4 will require lots more carding to consistently blend the colours together.

- When you have finished lay these out as in picture 3 so that you know where to start spinning and in what order these mini batts should be spun. You will notice that I split the carded balls 2 and 4 into two mini batts, as previously described... I have done this purely so that I had smaller amounts on the wheel, or spindle at one time to work with... you may prefer to keep them as one larger ball.

- Pick up your first colour and start spinning... now because we are creating a swatch, I am not worried about truly consistent yarn, or aiming for a particular weight of yarn (4ply, dk, aran, etc.)

- When this colour is finished, join your second colour and then the third afterwards... until you have completed spinning all colours.

- You now have a bobbin, or spindle cop full of yarn.

- To ply this yarn and balance it (singles often bias when knit) I have chosen to Navajo ply.

When you have finished plying, let you yarn rest either on the spindle/bobbin or a niddy noddy for a day. This will help relax any areas of slight over spin. You are now able to set your yarn in the usual way.

Knit up a swatch and take a good look at how the swatch knits up. If you completed the earlier swatch, you will note that the swatch as seen in my picture above knits in a much more subtle effect of colour transition.

Now we can move onto pattern ideas.

## Pattern Ideas

I thought it might help to understand what sort of finished effects we could hope to achieve by making our own gradient yarns; where it be one yarn encompassing all colours, or separate skeins we have made to graduate a colour transition across a garment. To help illustrate some ideas I have turned to Ravelry.com.

All of these patterns show you that gradients are a wonderful way to express colour through our projects. Whilst some would be better with a more bold gradient, others benefit from a more subtle transition in colour.

The other great thing about creating your own gradient yarns from separate pre dyed colours, is that you can determine how much of each colour you use in your project, or how even the transitions are spaced.

The down side to creating your own gradients? Well, it can be a lot of work, a lot more work than buying in a hand dyed option.

## Fisherman's Cowl Pattern

This is a simple pattern using a faux gradient or hand dyed gradient…. I have chosen a true gradient, but a progressive would also be fine.

This is a spin to knit pattern… its origin in design is based on a visit to Brixham.

**Skill Level** – Intermediate.

**Yarn** – 186g/157m, 8wpi bulky weight hand spun yarn. Alternatively you could try a commercial bulky weight. The gradient is made using lessons learned in the 'Faux' gradient conversation of the spinning series.

**Needles** – 6mm/10 US 60cm circulars.

**Finished Measurements** – Laying flat the cowl measures 12 inches by 12 inches (30.5cm)

**To Fit:** One size fits all.

**Ease** – None.

**Abbreviations:**
Sts – stitches
PM – Place marker
K – Knit
K2tog – Knit 2 together
YO – Yarn Over

**Directions –**
- Cast on 96sts, PM and join in the round (do not twist).
- 2x2 rib for 3 rows.

- ['K2tog, yo' repeat to end of row.
- K to end of row.]
- Repeat two rows from [ to ]. Continue until almost enough yarn left over to create final rib.
- 2x2 rib for 3 rows.
- Cast off using a stretchy bind off.

**Blocking:** I used a wet light spray block (lying flat), but nothing more.

<u>Cloisters Hat Pattern</u>

This is a simple pattern for a progressive gradient, but a true gradient would also work because the lace is very simple and on a larger scale.

This is a spin to knit pattern… it's origin in design is based on my local cathedral. I'm using my colour Poolside.

**Skill Level** – Intermediate.

**Yarn** – 100g/99m, 7wpi bulky weight handspun. Alternatively you could try a commercial bulky weight.

**Needles** – 6mm/10 US 40cm circulars, with 6mm double point needles to cast off.

**Finished Measurements** – Laying flat the brim measures 16" in circumference and the hat is 8 inches tall.

**To Fit:** 20 inch head circumference.

**Ease** – approx.. 4cm negative ease.

**Abbreviations:**
Sts – stitches
PM – Place marker
K – Knit
P – Purl
K1tbl – Knit 1 through the back loop
P2tog – Purl 2 together
Yo – Yarn Over
Sl1 – slip one
Sl1K2togPsso – Slip 1, knit 2 together, pass slip stitch over
K2Tog tbl – knit two stitches together, through the back loop

**Directions** – You will be knitting this hat inside out... I think it's an easier knit that way.

- Cast on 54sts and PM.
- 'P1, k1tbl' repeat to end. Repeat for 1 1/4 inches.
- 'P5, k1tbl' repeat to end. Repeat until total length is 2 inches.

Pattern:
- 'Yo, p2tog, p1, p2tog, yo, k1tbl'... Repeat to end.
- 'P5, k1tbl' repeat to end... Repeat to end.
- 'P1, yo, Sl1K2togPsso (forming the cloister pyramid), yo, p1, k1tbl'... Repeat to end.
- 'P5, k1tbl' repeat to end.
- 'P1, k1tbl' repeat to end. Repeat until measures 7 inches.

Decreases:

- 'P1, k1tbl, p1, k1 tbl, p2 tog' repeat to end.
- 'P1, k1tbl, p1, k2tog tbl' repeat to end.
- 'P1, k1tbl, p2tog' repeat to end.
- 'P1, k2tog tbl' repeat to end.
- 'P2tog' repeat to end.

Cut long tail and draw through centre of stitches to close top. Remember you are knitting inside out so finish on the side you have been knitting. Turn inside out and wear!

**Blocking:** You do not need to block this hat, as the negative ease will reshape the item when you wear it. However, you can lightly wet block it if you prefer.

## Designing Your Gradient Knits

Designing your own gradient knits is very rewarding way of working with colour. I want to use a few garment types to show you the differences between each gradient type and also how they might look on a finished garment.

I hope this will inspire you to start working with gradients more often.

### Hats

I thought it might be nice to start this by looking at the humble hat; a basic stockinette beanie with a rib brim. Why a hat? Well not only are they quick to knit, but you can use very simple ply techniques to utilise your gradient fibres.

*Before we go into this, please ignore my child-like colouring in... yes I did have full design training... I rather stupidly didn't perform today, LOL!*

Ok... So let's have a look at these two beanie hats..

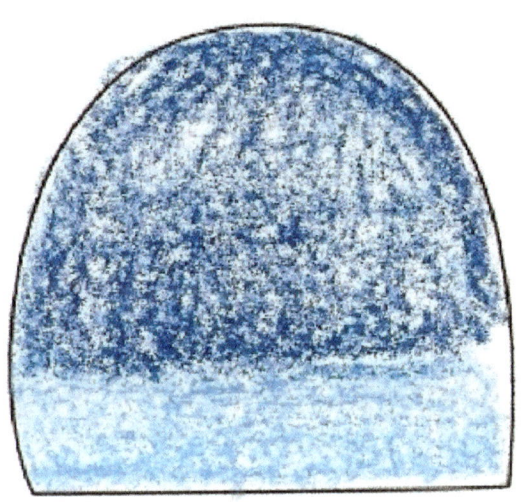 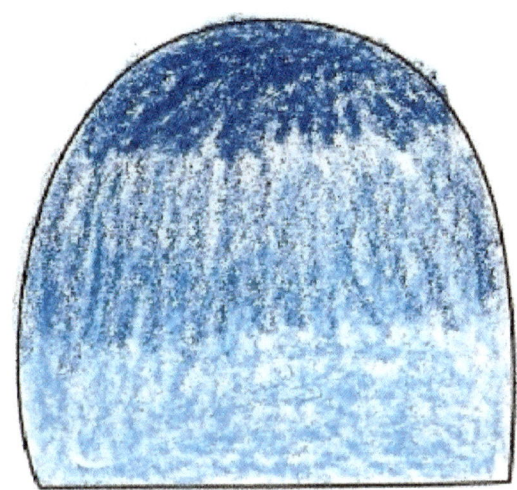

**Progressive**          **True**

One uses a progressive gradient idea (like the Cloisters pattern), where you have a very distinct line between colours. This could be accomplished by creating your own faux gradient, or buying a progressive dyed braid of fibre. Navajo ply would be a great way to keep those colours separate, especially on a faux spin.

Why would I use a progressive gradient for a hat? Tipping, is my answer... 'Tipping' refers to a band of colour usually at the edge of a garment that acts as a trim without having to change stitch detail. On a hat you could design your yarn to knit the ribbing in one colour before you switch to the next colour in the gradient. This would take a bit of working out if you wanted a specific rib height, but you could always play with finishing your rib a bit earlier if the tipping colour changes to the full body colour sooner than you thought.

The other hat uses a true gradient. With this method you would get a good stretch of one colour merging into another. I recommend a standard two ply as the easiest method of ply choice.

Why would I use a true gradient for a hat? This is more of a styling choice, in that a gradient basic beanie could be much more interesting to knit than a plain one... it gives a bit of depth to a stockinette knit.

Shawls

There are many shawl designs out there; from top down or bottom up triangles, sideways shawls, crescent trim edge shawls... so many choices and so many different ways a gradient could affect the finished look of your knitting.

We are going to look at a basic triangle shape and consider how the colour will play out by knitting different gradient types and then in different directions.

The first shawls I have rather crudely drawn up use the basics discussed in under the hats section and show the distinct colour change of a progressive gradient and the true graduation of a true gradient. Here you can see how the different styles of gradient spin will affect your finished knit.

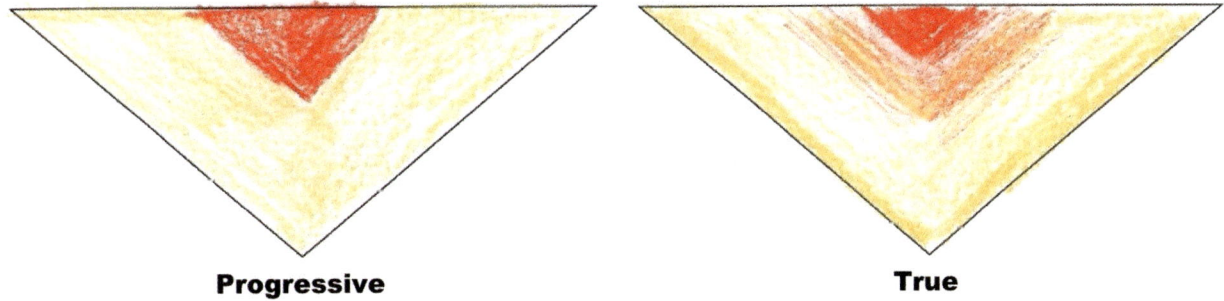

**Progressive**                    **True**

Given this, let's look at choosing or designing our shawl pattern around different directional knitting; top down, border contrast, or sideways knits... For this I'm using a progressive colour choice, purely to show the difference in colour more easily.

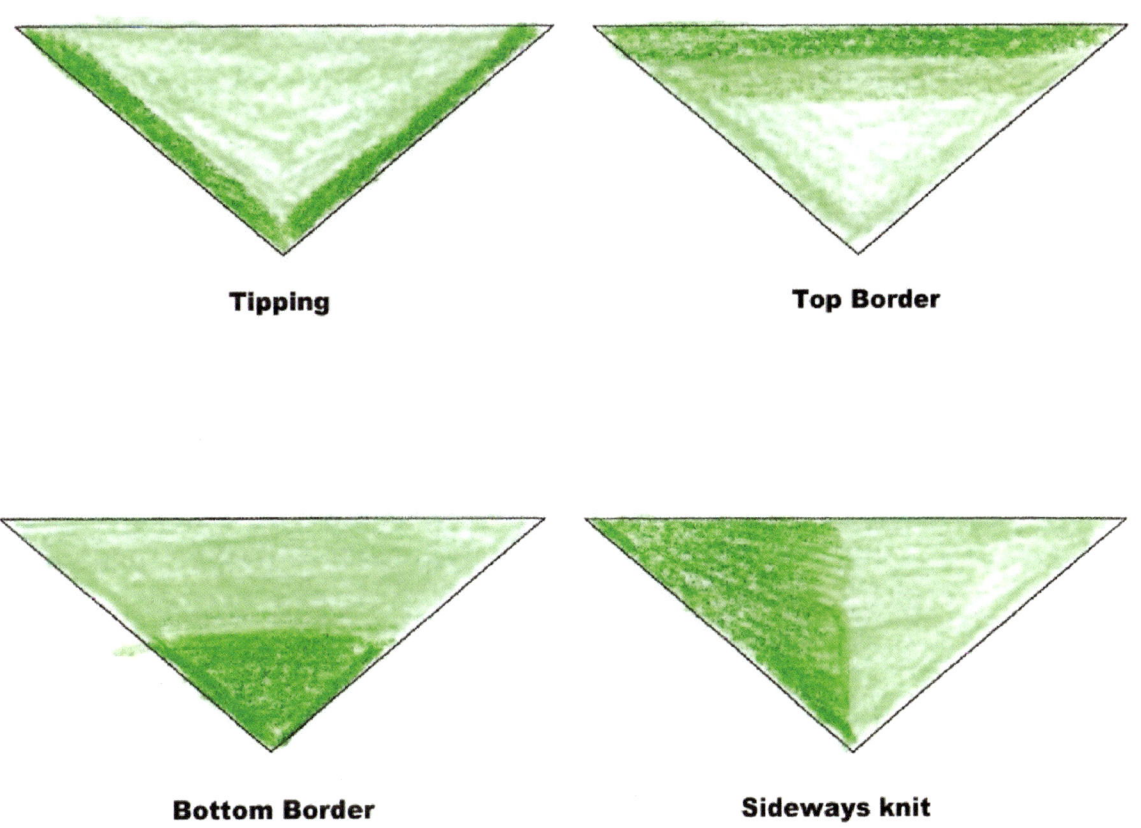

**Tipping**                        **Top Border**

**Bottom Border**                  **Sideways knit**

This is all just playing with colour, we haven't started to think about pattern and stitch design! I think it is clear to say that spinning your gradient yarn and making the choice between a true or progressive colour change is only the start of the design fun.

Socks

Socks have become very popular to spin for with so many choices in hand dyed fibres out there, gradients are one of the easiest ways to create unique socks that anyone, any age would love.

The best ply traditionally for socks is a standard three ply (not Navajo, as it's not always strong enough at the chain joins). So when you are separating your fibres you would need to be very careful to control your spin, making sure that if you want a progressive colour change, you keep those colours as separate as possible to keep the distinct nature of the overall gradient.

With this in mind it is probably easier to consider spinning a true gradient, then any inconsistencies in your singles, when plied will matter little and in fact aid the diffusion of colour change along the gradient.

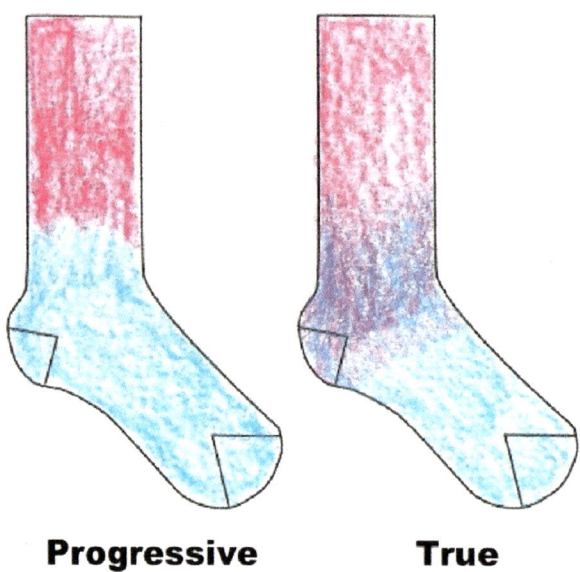

**Progressive**          **True**

There are also other design choices that can help you crate a unique sock... consider things like contrast heel and toes.

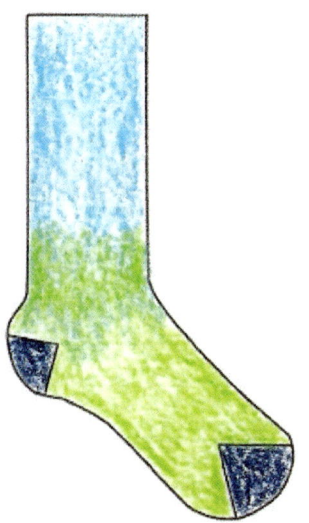

## Creating Different Effects with Gradients

I want us to start looking at different ways to use our gradient yarns and create different look knits.

So far we have discussed gradients, different types, how to use them, pattern ideas and ways to spin for them... what if a gradient could become a different form of colour technique, like a stripe?

Well let's talk... Stripes!

### Stripes

For stripes you don't need to use a hand dyed gradient specifically, you can of course create your own faux stripe from separate stash colours, but for the purpose of this discussion let's stick to looking at hand dyed gradients... in this case a progressive gradient for clear definition of colours.

Here we have two stripe swatches, one that has large stripe repeats and the other has quick changing mini repeats of colour.

How do we create these from one single braid of gradient fibre?

I'm starting with my colour Heatwave.

Let's look at the larger stripe repeats first...

Here I split my braid length ways into three roughly equal parts (of course it's good to note that they will never be truly accurate splitting this way as you can see in the swatch). I then spun them end to end and Navajo plied the yarn. Knitting up it gives me a stripe effect.

For the mini stripes (above) I tore the braids into piles of the two colours and then laid them out next to each other. I started spinning the red, then the yellow and then red again and so on. Again this isn't an accurate spin as you can see in the swatch, but it does give a rustic stripe effect when Navajo plied.

It is important to remember scale in your stripe spinning... for these swatches I used 100g, so 50g per swatch. 50g of colour has given me a very small scale of stripe to my yarn and so if I knitted say a cowl, the colours may 'pool' (merge together in waves of the same colour from row to row) or create a 'space dye' effect instead of the stripe I desired. So for a cowl I would be better to create my yarn from a larger amount of fibre to start with, say 100-150g, maybe even 200g (based on a Navajo ply). This would give me a better scale of stripe effect for my chosen project. _Swatching is key here._

Scale is also important to remember if we wanted to go larger still and knit a sweater for example. Here we might consider gradient spinning each of our 100g braids individually and then adding them end to end with the next yarn as we knit. This will create a stripe across the body of our garment... remember to watch your sleeves though, as the smaller width will elongate the stripe effect and it will look significantly different to the main body. In this case it might be better to consider just striping the body and using just one colour on the sleeves... unless of course different widths of stripe is your design choice.

One last and important thing to think about is construction... if you are knitting in the round or an item (like a hat) that tapers off to a smaller scale or finish point then stripes will start doing different things, like pooling. So if stripes are what you are after then consider 'piece' construction, for example knitting the front and back of your garment separately. This should help keep those stripes even. If you have a wider neckline, or are definite on a yoke top down sweater then you may consider the top yoke in one colour and then moving to stripes as you get to the body. Lots to think about!

Having said all of these stripes are a wonderful thing to work with and if you don't feel comfortable using the gradient you bought as a gradient, then why not consider a different type of spin?

Marls

So far we have looked at gradients and stripes... now we will concentrate on diffusion techniques. In this case 'Marls'.

For this you don't need to use a hand dyed gradient specifically, you can of course create your own faux gradient from separate stash colours, but for the purpose of this discussion let's stick to looking at hand dyed gradients... in this specific case a progressive gradient for clear definition of colours.

Here we have two marl swatches, one that has large striped marl repeats and the other has a true marl effect.

How do we create these from one single braid of gradient fibre?

I'm starting with my colour Creek.

Let's look at the larger stripe marl repeats first...

Here I split my braid length ways into two roughly equal parts. I spun the first half (in the braid above) as one single starting with the brown and working towards the blue.

The second half I split again lengthways into three roughly equal parts. I spun this single starting with one of the balls above from brown to blue, then joined the next ball from brown to blue and then the third. This is called FRACTAL SPINNING. I plied using a standard two plying technique.

When this yarn was knit up you can see I had a stripe effect, but more diffused than we saw in our stripe conversation. This would be great for fibres with very different hues of colour that you might otherwise be a little afraid to wear... diffusion, or blending allows a softer knit effect.

Creating long marled stripes from a gradient top

by Sara's Texture Crafts

For the true marl effect swatch above I created a batt on my drum carder (you can hand card rolags too if you prefer). I started by tearing the braid of Creek into several pieces so that I could layer the batt with smaller layers of blue, then brown, then blue, and so on. Carding on the drum carder helped to diffuse the colours further, so that when I spun my single (before Navajo plying) the colours would be blended.

When knitted you can see how the colours have truly blended giving us a true marl effect... quite different to the original gradient.

It is of course important to say here that the number of times you pass the batt through the drum carder will effect how blended your batt becomes. Always play with small swatches before you start on a larger project, because blending 'too far' could produce a muddy effect.

*[A special note here... if you'd like to learn more about spinning with batts and how to make them, check out my new series coming 2015/16!]*

## Other Spinning Ideas

I'm sure if you are creative there are many other ways you can use gradient dyed fibres to create unique effects in your yarn. Here are a few ideas off of the top of my head;

1. Spin against a solid, or semi solid shade. This will elongate your colour gradient length for larger projects and add a marl type effect through 'Barber Poling' (each strand of the yarn differ in colour).

2. Spin against a novelty yarn for a textured marl effect.

3. Spin a cool gradient against a warm gradient. This should make colours pop in your yarn.

## Art Yarns

Art yarns are a great way to add texture to knits and also to create bold statements in smaller pieces, like jewellery.

If you'd like to get into art yarn spinning I recommend Jacey Bogg's book, Spin Art: Mastering the Craft of Spinning Textured Yarn

## Tips on Buying Gradient Braids

Here is my tip list for buying gradients either on-line, or at shows;

- Think colours… do they suit your skin tone?

- If the colour is not 'you', but you still like it then think smaller accent knits, or smaller projects like mitts, or socks. Or think about spinning for stripes or marls.

- What are you spinning for? Larger or smaller projects? If so how much do you need?

- What ply will you be spinning? Navajo… if so you will need more fibre.

- If you are creating an art yarn, you may also choose to get more fibre to play with.

- If you are trying a new ply structure or creative technique then opt for a forgiving fibre, like a long staple BFL, or an 'easy draft' Shetland.

## Conclusion

Gradients are a wonderfully versatile and clever way to expand your spinning arsenal of design techniques. They can easily turn any colourway into something uniquely you.

Don't be afraid to experiment!

Happy Crafting,

Sara x

www.sarastexturecrafts.com

## Further Reading and Resources

Website: www.sarastexturecrafts.com

Blog: www.craftsoftexture.com

Ravelry Group: I have started a Ravelry thread in the group for anyone who wants to share and chat about their gradient experiments.
http://www.ravelry.com/discuss/saras-texture-crafts/topics/2948721

Video link to Navajo ply - Sarah Anderson at Interweave.
https://www.youtube.com/watch?v=JmlwtojLXl8

Jacey boggs book - Spin Art: Mastering the Craft of Spinning Textured Yarn

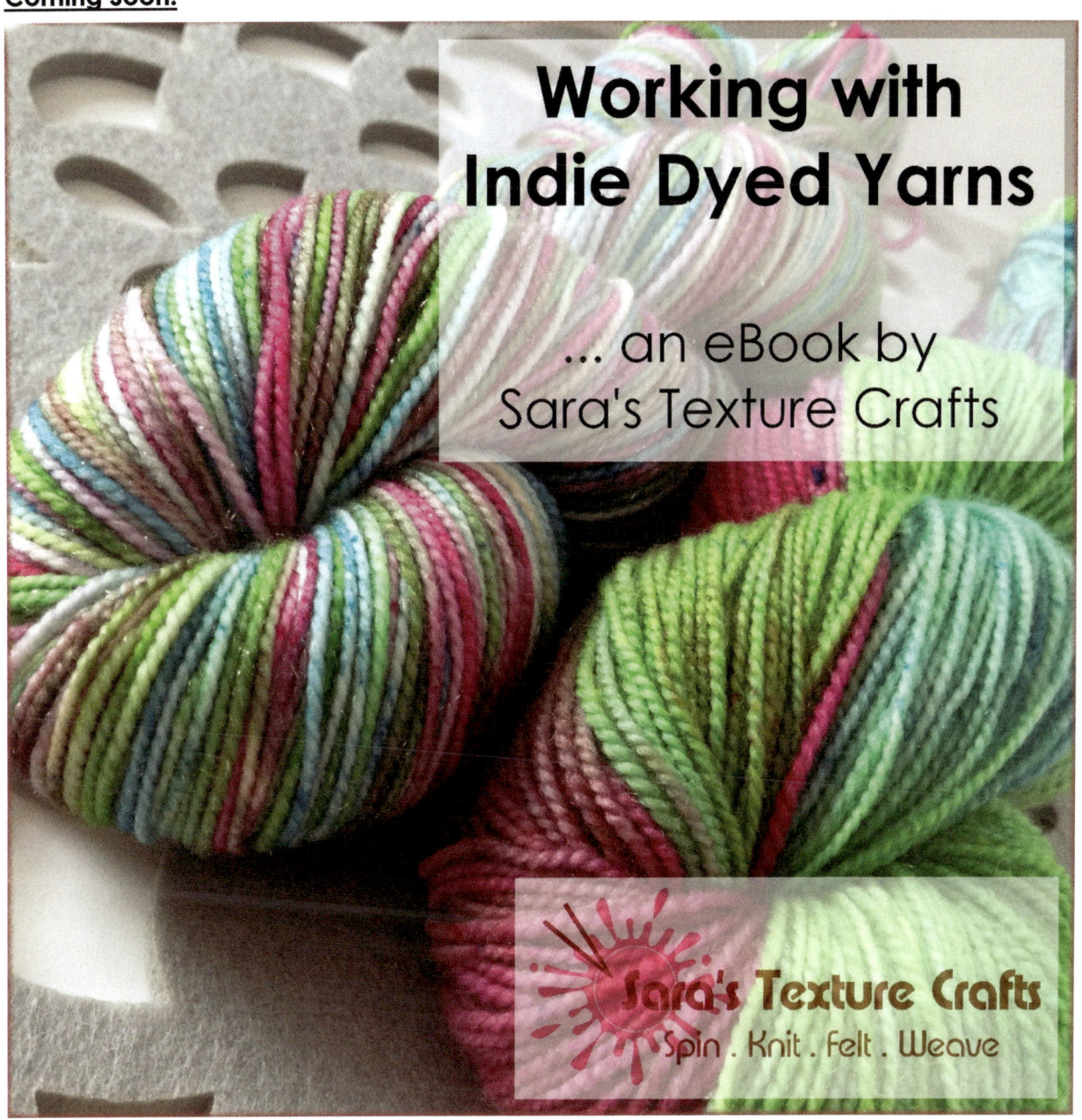

Working with
Indie Dyed Yarns

... an eBook by
Sara's Texture Crafts

Sara's Texture Crafts
Spin . Knit . Felt . Weave

Printed in Great Britain
by Amazon